Pianoworks
Collection 1

compiled and arranged by
Janet and Alan Bullard

MUSIC DEPARTMENT

OXFORD
UNIVERSITY PRESS

OXFORD
UNIVERSITY PRESS

Great Clarendon Street, Oxford OX2 6DP, England
198 Madison Avenue, New York, NY, 10016, USA

Oxford University Press is a department of the University of Oxford.
It furthers the University's aim of excellence in research, scholarship,
and education by publishing worldwide

Oxford is a registered trademark of Oxford University Press
in the UK and in certain other countries

9 10

ISBN 978–0–19–335583–5

Music and text origination by
Barnes Music Engraving Ltd., East Sussex.
Printed in Great Britain on acid-free paper by
Halstan & Co. Ltd., Amersham, Bucks.

Contents

Allegro
Last movement of Trumpet Concerto

Joseph Haydn (1732–1809)
arr. editors

Haydn wrote his Trumpet Concerto in 1796, and it was one of the first works to use the keyed trumpet—the predecessor of the modern valve trumpet. In this arrangement of the main theme from the last movement the melody is shared between the hands.

Salangadou

Trad. Creole
arr. editors

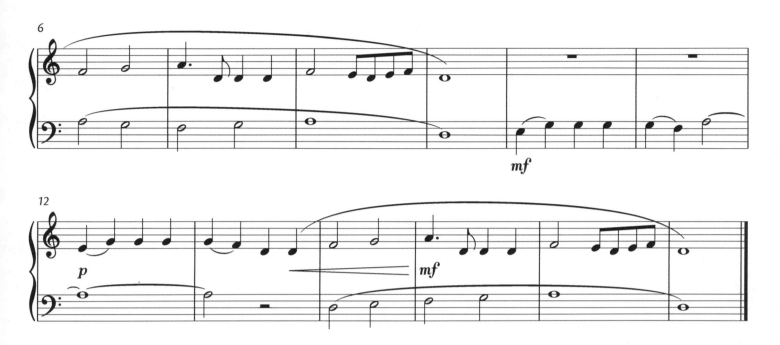

Legato and expressive playing will create the melancholy mood required in this traditional Creole song from New Orleans, in which a mother laments the death of her daughter.

La Volta

Anon. English (*c.*1600)
arr. editors

This energetic dance was popular all over Europe in the seventeenth century. A contemporary description explains that the man puts his left arm around his partner's waist and the right arm beneath her bust, then helps her to leap into the air with a push from his left thigh, while both partners rapidly turn. It was banned by the French court for its risks to both 'honour and health'!

The Trout

Franz Schubert (1797–1828)
arr. editors

Schubert was a prolific songwriter, and 'The Trout' ('Die Forelle'), one of his most popular songs, was also the theme of his 'Trout' Quintet. It tells the sad tale of a carefree, playful fish, who is soon to be caught by a cruel fisherman.

Minuetto

Charles Wilton
(b. c.1761)

The Minuet originated as a French aristocratic dance, and its stately and elegant style made it one of the most popular dances of the seventeenth and eighteenth centuries. Charles Wilton, the composer of this minuet, lived in Gloucester, studied in Italy, and later became the leader of the orchestra of the Three Choirs Festival.

Alas, summer is ending

Neidhart von Reuenthal (c.1190–c.1240)
arr. editors

Based on a medieval German courtly song, this piece contrasts the sadness of the end of summer (in the first section) with bitter anger towards an unfaithful lover (at the end).

Belle qui tiens ma vie

Anon.
Arbeau's *Orchésographie* (1588)
arr. editors

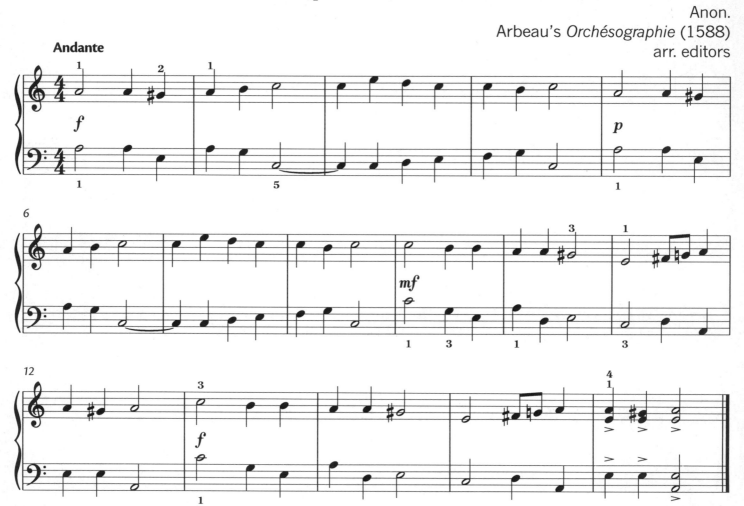

This song, popularized in the twentieth century by its inclusion in Peter Warlock's *Capriol Suite*, was originally published in a collection of dances by the French cleric Thoinot Arbeau. The words read: 'Beautiful one, who holds my life captive in your eyes, come to my aid or I must die'. It would have been performed with a steady drumbeat underpinning the rhythm.

Horn Fanfare
from the 'Water Music'

George Frideric Handel
(1685–1759)

Handel spent much of his working life in England, and the Water Music was written for a party on the Thames for George I. The musicians performed from a barge following the royal barge, and the King enjoyed it so much he asked for the hour-long work to be played three times. Imagine this horn duet being played in the distance the first time, then close by in the repeat.

Andante

August Müller
(1767–1817)

Müller was the director of music at St Thomas's Church, Leipzig, as was J. S. Bach before him. He was a flautist, organist, and pianist. Many of his compositions were forward-looking in style and were highly esteemed by Beethoven.

Kemp's Jig

Anon. (c.1600)
arr. editors

This anonymous dance celebrates the actor William Kemp, *who* danced a morris dance from *London to Norwich* in 1600 and wrote an account of it *called* 'Kemps Nine Daies Wonder'. It is full of variety and **musical** contrast, reflecting the energy of the morris dance.

Melody in C
from *ABC du Piano*

Félix Le Couppey
(1811–87)

Le Couppey was Professor of Piano at the Paris Conservatoire and wrote much educational music including *ABC du Piano* (1859), which contains this piece. The right-hand melody sings beautifully above the left-hand accompaniment.

Iona Boat Song

Trad. Scottish
arr. editors

Legend has it that this was the tune to which Scottish kings were rowed to their final resting place on the sacred isle of Iona. Legato pedalling will add to the haunting atmosphere, and holding the pedal down for the last four bars enables the sound to float into the distance.

Fiddler on the Roof

Jerry Bock (b. 1928)
arr. editors

Fiddler on the Roof is a musical set in a Jewish community in pre-revolutionary Russia. This theme from the overture makes use of the characteristic scale patterns of klezmer music.

Lullaby

Charles Villiers Stanford (1852–1924)
adapted editors

Irish-born Stanford was a professor of composition at London's Royal College of Music and was a fine composer of symphonic and choral music, eclipsed only by his near-contemporary Elgar. The unhurried swaying opening bars suggest the gentle rocking of a cradle.

Menuet in F
from L. Mozart's *Nannerl-Notenbuch*

Anon. 18th cent.

This piece is taken from a collection compiled by Leopold Mozart for his eight-year-old daughter, Nannerl—an excellent musician whose fame was overshadowed by that of her brother, Wolfgang Amadeus.

The Policeman's Song

from *The Pirates of Penzance*

Arthur Sullivan (1842–1900)

arr. editors

Moderato: pompously

Gilbert and Sullivan's well-known operetta *The Pirates of Penzance* is the setting for this witty duet between the Sergeant and his chorus of Policemen, who obediently echo the last few words of each phrase (always marked *f* with accents). This piece should be 'hammed up' as much as possible!

In dulci jubilo

14th-cent. German
arr. editors

In 1328 Heinrich Seuse, a German Dominican monk, had a dream in which angels were singing and dancing this carol. It has been popular ever since and arranged by many composers, including J. S. Bach. The Latin words mean 'In sweet jubilation'.

Moderato

Anton Diabelli
(1781–1858)

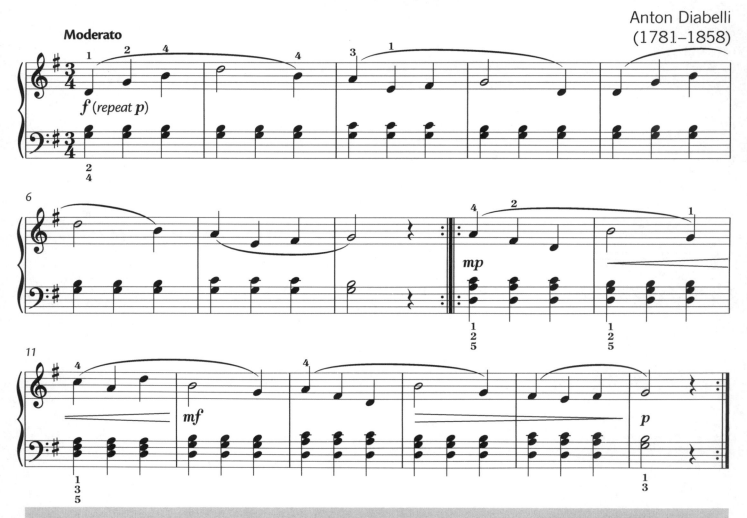

Diabelli was an Austrian piano teacher and music publisher who wrote a large quantity of church and educational music. This piece needs careful balancing between the hands to ensure that the melody sings out over the left-hand chords.

Thin Ice

Alan Bullard
(b. 1947)

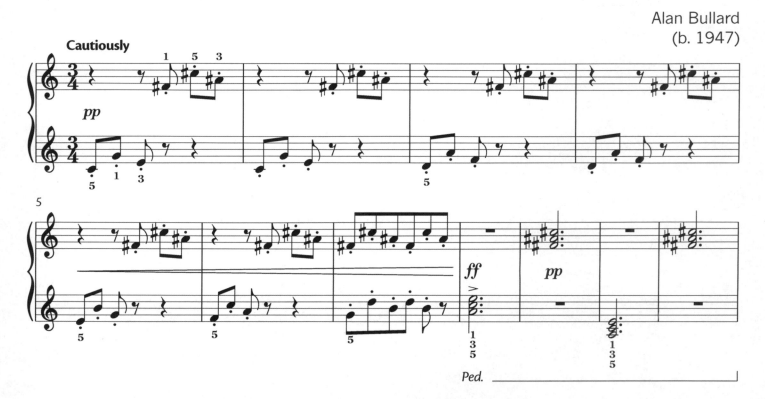

This piece is not as difficult as it looks! The right hand always plays black notes while the left hand always plays white notes. Although the hands move right across the keyboard, they always remain in the five-finger position, and the right hand mostly sits above the left hand. The brittle effect of the opening staccato quavers leads into sliding and overlapping sonorities emphasized by the use of the sustaining pedal.

Etre jaloux de son camarade qui a une grosse tête
from *Peccadilles importunes*

Erik Satie
(1866–1925)

This strange and haunting piece (translated as 'Being jealous of your big-headed friend') by the composer of the *Gymnopédies* shows Satie anticipating the repetitive minimalist style of recent times (compare with Skempton's 'Quavers' later in the book). Very much of their own time, though, are the surrealist comments on the original score of the music, translated as follows: 'He who is jealous isn't happy . . . I knew a little boy who was envious of his parrot . . . He would have wished to know his lessons as well as the parrot knew his'. Although these comments may not help us specifically to interpret the music, they do suggest a somewhat remote approach which could be achieved with no dynamic contrast and evenly flowing quavers, allowing the simplicity of the music to speak for itself.

Adagio
Second movement of Clarinet Concerto

Wolfgang Amadeus Mozart (1756–91)
arr. editors

Mozart wrote this beautiful and serene movement during the troubled final months of his life. In the concerto the solo clarinet plays each section first, and the repeats are played by the full orchestra.

Street Beat

Alan Bullard
(b. 1947)

With pride and poise

This jazz-/rock-influenced piece is driven by the steady crotchet pulse, and the off-beat accents and dynamic contrasts help to emphasize the mood.

Aura Lee
(Love me tender)

George R. Poulton (1828–67)
arr. editors

'Aura Lee' is a sentimental ballad from the American Civil War and was popularized by Elvis Presley in the film *Love me Tender*, where it appears with different words. The opening part of the melody is played by the left hand while the right hand provides a gentle accompaniment.

Autumn Leaves

Joseph Kosma (1905–69)
arr. editors

Joseph Kosma was a Hungarian musician who in the 1930s was exiled to Paris, where he worked as a cabaret pianist and film composer. 'Les feuilles mortes' ('Autumn Leaves') was first sung by Yves Montand in the film *Les Portes de la Nuit* (1946) and, taken up by Juliette Greco and Edith Piaf, soon became an international hit.

Quavers

Howard Skempton
(b. 1947)

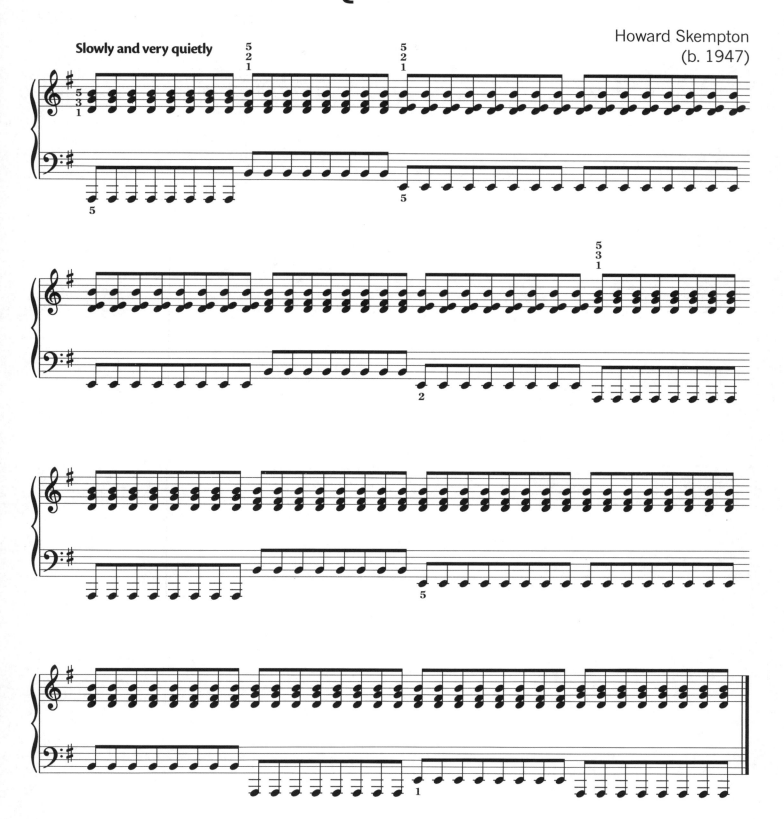

Howard Skempton's elegantly pared-down musical language is seen by many as a breath of fresh air in an age of much musical complexity. 'Quavers' is the first of a number of similar studies; although the music is essentially in $\frac{4}{4}$, the lack of time signature or bar-lines suggests that the quavers should be played absolutely evenly, with no perceptible accents. Legato pedalling with each chord change will enhance the mood of stillness.

Waltz
from *The Sleeping Beauty*

Pyotr Il'yich Tchaikovsky (1840–93)
arr. editors

In this graceful waltz from Tchaikovsky's famous ballet *The Sleeping Beauty* the dancers twirl on the stage as the music rises to a crescendo of excitement in the last line. In this arrangement the melody moves from left hand to right, suggesting the sound of cellos followed by violins.

Rustic Dance

August Müller
(1767–1817)

With its $\frac{6}{8}$ pulse and energetic melody, 'Rustic Dance' captures the flavour of a lively eighteenth-century country dance.

Whistle down the Wind

Andrew Lloyd Webber (b. 1948)
arr. editors

Whistle down the Wind is a musical that tells of the clash between tradition, prejudice, and youthful innocence in 1950s America. This title song evokes a feeling of dream-like nostalgia.

Longing
from *I begin to play*

Feliks Rybicki
(1899–1978)

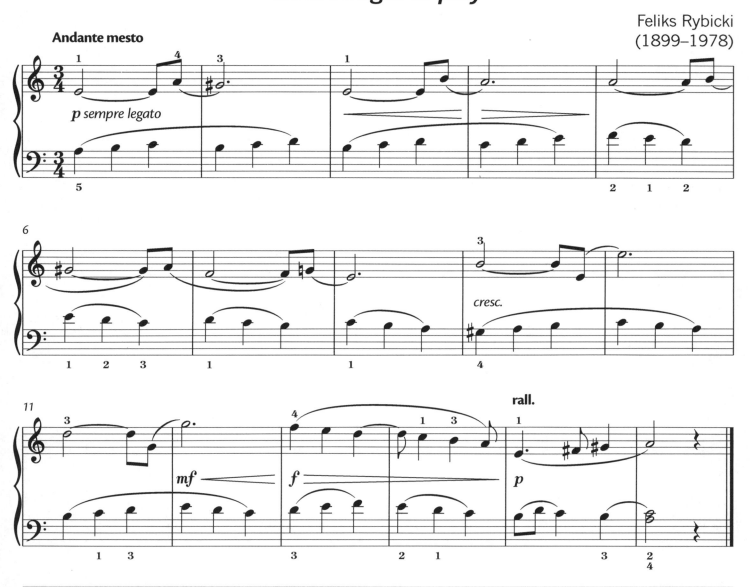

The Polish composer and conductor Feliks Rybicki wrote many characterful miniatures for piano, as well as larger-scale works. This gentle piece has an expressive melodic line with a flowing accompaniment, and the dynamic markings give it character and shape.

See, the Conquering Hero Comes
from *Judas Maccabaeus*

George Frideric Handel (1685–1759)
arr. editors

This collection finishes with the triumphant chorus from the oratorio *Judas Maccabaeus*. The choir sings: 'See, the conquering hero comes, sound the trumpets, beat the drums. Sports prepare, the laurels bring, songs of triumph to him sing'. An ideal piece for many a celebratory occasion!

ISBN: 978-0-19-335582-8

Pianoworks

BOOK 1

Janet and Alan Bullard

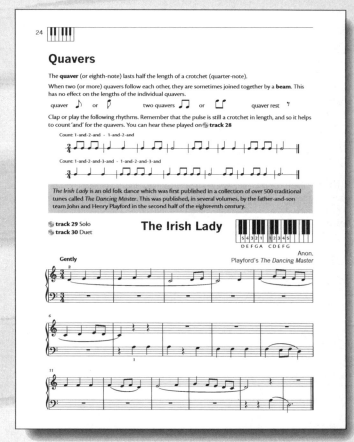

If you've ever wanted to play the piano, look no further! Whether you have some experience or just a desire to learn, *Pianoworks Book 1* provides all you need to get started.

✦ Perfect for the adult or older beginner

✦ Well-paced, with plenty of examples and exercises

✦ New topics carefully introduced in a logical progression

✦ Appealing and accessible pieces

✦ Keyboard diagrams help the student find their way around the piano

✦ CD with performances, backing tracks, and exercises

For the older beginner